R. J. B. Willis

How to
reduce&survive
STRESS

First published 2010

Copyright © 2010 Autumn House
Publishing (Europe) Ltd.

British Library Cataloguing in Publication Data.
A catalogue record for this book is available
from the British Library.

ISBN 978-1-906381-83-7

Published by Autumn House, Grantham, Lincolnshire.
Designed by Abigail Murphy.
Printed in Thailand.

Unless otherwise indicated, Bible verses have been
taken from the *New International Version* of the Bible
(Hodder and Stoughton).

Other version used, indicated by initials:

GNB = *Good News Bible* (Collins)

Oh, the nerves, the nerves;
the mysteries of this machine
called man! Oh the little
that unhinges it, poor
creatures that we are!
Charles Dickens

Stress is a special kind of transaction between a person and his/her environment.

Defining stress

Stress is the state manifested
by a specific syndrome
which consists of all the
non-specifically inducted
changes within a
biologic system.

Dr Hans Selye

Everywhere stress

Stressors are omnipresent in human existence. In response to a stressor, the organism responds with a state of tension.

Aaron Antonovsky

Escaping anxiety

I have constantly tried to single
out one end in human actions
which all men unanimously hold
as good and which they all
seek. I have found only this: The
aim of escaping anxiety. . . . Not
only have I discovered that all
humanity considers this good
and desirable, but also . . . no
one is moved to act or moved to
speak a single word who does
not hope by means of this
action or word to release
anxiety from his spirit.

Ali Ibn Hazm of Cordova (11th century)

Universal stress

Everyone is subjected every day to stress of one kind or another. It can blight happiness, or stimulate anyone to give of his best. It cannot be 'cured' but it can be controlled.

F. E. Graham-Bonnalie

Starting young

Children have less manoeuvrability to deal with their stressors than adults. Starting with their entrance to school, even relatively relaxed children have a great deal to handle. All at once they have to face a structured, confined environment, discipline, competitive peer pressure, and teacher and parental pressure and expectations. Their little bodies start trying to adapt to these demands, using the same mechanisms grown-up bodies use.

Dr Liz Stroebel

Stress is a necessary and important ingredient to life.

We call the things that cause stress – although different in origin and intensity – **stressors.**

Stressors include basic feelings such as *hunger*, *thirst* and *tiredness*. Without these feelings we would not go looking for food, drink and rest, which help to keep our bodies alive, fit and well.

... not all stress is bad. When stress is positive, we call it a 'challenge'. But when stress is negative, we call it a 'crisis'.... One person's crisis may be another person's challenge.

Len D. McMillan

Degrees of feeling

... there could be a large
measure of agreement among
people that certain experiences
or phenomena are stressors.
Yet at the same time they might
well differ considerably in the
extent to which they personally
experience such stressors.

Aaron Antonovsky

Eustress vs distress

eustress ———————— *distress*
stress continuum

eustress describes happy,
delightful, challenging forms of
stress and is always positive

distress is the more accurate
description of the negative
effects that we usually call
stress

Stress also includes the heart-rending emotional strains of bereavement or divorce, and other long-term problems giving rise to anxieties.

Stress provides the stimuli to physical, mental, social and spiritual growth as the various needs are met.

Self-adaptation

If the person who is subjected
to stress is ultimately to survive
in an undamaged condition
then his reactions must be such
that he is capable of adapting
himself to the stress exerted
upon him.

F. E. Graham-Bonnalie

Getting to grips with the problem

One must first understand the cause of the difficulty, innovate and weigh alternative solutions, consider workable resources, devise a plan of action, try out that plan, and modify it.

Stuart Palmer

Predictable responses

Although we each react in different ways to stressors, as individuals we start to react in much the same way each time we face stress.

Our physical and behavioural responses become predictable, automatic and habitual. In the long term these can cause negative health consequences.

Change and vulnerability

The greater the life change or adaptive requirement, the greater the vulnerability or lowering of resistance to disease, and the more serious the disease that does develop. . . . Thus, the concept of life change appears to have relevance to the causation of disease, time of onset of disease and severity of disease.

T. H. Holmes, M. Masuda

Withdrawals only

Our reserves of adaptation
energy might be compared to
an inherited bank account from
which we can make withdrawals
but to which we apparently
cannot make deposits.

Thus, adaptability should be
used wisely and sparingly
rather than squandered.
Dr Hans Selye

Stress is viewed as involving four elements:

- *a threat*
- *felt need for action*
- *uncertainty*
- *an emotional response* (more often based on anxiety or fear)

Breakdown has four
crucial facets:

- pain
- functional limitations
- prognostic implications
- action implications

Aaron Antonovsky

Disintegration of personality

... as stress arousal continues,
deteriorative effects are
noticeable in all aspects of
performance, of judgement, and
of relations with others and with
oneself.

Tendencies toward rigidity of response, inflexibility, inability to profit from experience and to use new information, inability to shift when shifting is necessary or to persevere when required, suspiciousness, increase in hostility, irritability, increase in errors, and decrease in speed of performance all appear.

C. N. Cofer, M. H. Appley

There are some people who are constant worriers, living on their nerves. They increasingly react to stress in a predictable way and develop personality characteristics that determine their response.

This reaction is called *trait anxiety*, and if these behaviours are not modified or changed they can lead to *acute* and *chronic* physical conditions.

Worry is a rocking horse.

It gets nowhere.

Stress perception

Perception of stress is
made at two levels:

• *conscious*, in which the
faculties of the mind are
brought to bear on the stressor.

• *unconscious*, a more
automatic response having a
physical effect, so preparing the
body to deal with the stressor.

The key to the development of these stimuli lies in how the individual *perceives* and *reacts* to the stressors.

If the perception of the stressor is distorted for whatever reason, then the reaction is not likely to be appropriate.

A state of preparedness

The duration of the readiness and degree of the response will depend on the nature and severity of the stressor. The conscious assessment can or will overrule the unconscious appraisal and modify the physical response being made – hence the importance of an accurate perception of the stressor.

Different reactions

Imagine a child walking along a street with a parent. They pass a gate behind which is a big dog jumping and barking. The child is frightened and fearful as to what will happen. The parent, on the other hand, has noticed that the dog is tied up, and that the gate is too high for the dog to jump over, so is not worried about the situation.

Both have faced the same stressor – the dog – but their reactions have been different. The parent calms the child and all is well.

Sensing the stressor

The senses of sight, hearing,
touch, taste and smell provide
the brain with the data
necessary to make a judgement
and reaction to the stressor and
are channelled via the
hypothalamus (in the centre of
the brain) and the *pituitary
gland* (the master-gland of the
body).

The pituitary gland produces a substance called *adrenocorticotrophic hormone (ACTH)* which is carried to the adrenal glands (one on top of both kidneys).

ACTH stimulates the outer layer *(cortex)* of the adrenals to produce *corticosteroids*, and inner layer *(medulla)* to secrete *adrenaline*.

On alert

The effect of this chemistry on the body is immediate. The pulse becomes rapid as the heart beats faster; the breathing also becomes rapid as the heart demands more oxygen for the blood and the muscles become tense and 'alert', ready for action. This condition is often referred to as the *'fight or flight'* stage.

Return to normal

In a short while, depending on the nature and intensity of the stressor, all of these symptoms subside and the body returns to normal. Your body has been through a cycle called the *general arousal system*, which consists of the *alarm* stage, followed by a period of *resistance*, and then *exhaustion*.

Stress and physical health

If we are continual worriers the *general arousal system* has to work overtime and instead of helping quickly becomes a hindrance to our health.

We might start to get recurring headaches, high blood pressure, heart disease, mental ill-health, ulcers of the stomach and intestines, or arthritis and so on.

Perceptions of stress

from different points of view:

Air traffic controller – a
problem of concentration
Athlete – muscular tension
Biochemist – a purely
chemical event
Businessperson – frustration
or emotional tension

Change as a resource

... change is an inevitable part of all living things; change happens anyway. Our choice is whether to just let it happen or to embrace, guide and plan the kinds of change we want for ourselves.

Pete Bradshaw

The *intensity* of the reaction is proportional to the magnitude of the *perceived* danger or threat.

Emotional response

Many stressors are outside of our control, but there are others we can do something about. Foremost are the stressors caused by our lifestyle and our own thinking processes. These latter include: *desire for approval, envy, frustration, guilt, hate, irrational fears, jealousy, oversensitivity, resentment, self-centredness, sorrow, worry* and so on.

State vs trait anxiety

The condition of increasing and decreasing these physical changes is called *state anxiety* and, because these changes are only temporary, it is further defined as a *transitory emotional state*. This is the normal and natural response to various stress situations that we face.

Out of kilter!

. . . radical change and
instability are, by their nature,
not conducive to a strong sense
of coherence.

Aaron Antonovsky

Experience is not what happens
to a man. It is what a man does
with what happens to him.
Aldous Huxley

You don't have to suffer
continual chaos in
order to grow.
John C. Lilly

Sudden changes

'Future shock' ... the shattering
stress and disorientation that
we induce in individuals by
subjecting them to too much
change in too short a time.
Alvin Toffler

Change and crisis

Self-manufactured stressors are built up over a period of time. Other emotional stressors come in an instant, sometimes devastatingly. The name given to the pattern of progress by which we work through these stressors is called the *change and crisis sequence*.

The change and crisis sequence

The sequence has four phases, each with its own characteristics:

1. *Impact*
2. *Withdrawal – Confusion*
3. *Adjustment*
4. *Reconstruction – Reconciliation*

Although the phases are defined, in practice there is much overlapping of the characteristics, and the time factor of each varies with the stressor and its intensity. Progress is not always in a straight line through the phases and may be more like a swinging pendulum.

Those close to the stressed person may also have to work through the sequence but to a lesser degree.

Understanding anxiety

... anxiety is that form of
vigilance which occurs after
one has encountered a danger,
problem or opportunity but
before one has become aware
of its precise nature and thus
before one knows whether one
is still on familiar territory.

Charles Rycroft

Using anxiety

... the development and
toleration of ... anxiety is not
only inevitable but desirable
both as a stimulus to early
infantile development and as an
essential prerequisite for the
construction of adequate
defences in all danger
situations.
E. R. Zetzel

Fears

If we were really honest with
ourselves, we would admit to
holding a number of fears.
These can be rational or
irrational, depending on their
source.

We might fear the possibility
of ill-health, personal
loss or unemployment.
Included in these very real
fears are factors like loss of:

income, skills and activities, role and identity, time structures, social life and relationships, and our sense of purpose.

The stress caused by these factors leads to psychological and physical symptoms, which, if not dealt with, may compound the problem of ill-health. Family tensions and marital conflicts might arise.

Phobias

Fears held on to can turn into neurotic reactions. Neurotic reactions are of two types: *anxiety* and *phobia*.

Anxiety – may result from an unknown cause, in which case it is said to be *free floating*. The person is aware of anxieties but is unable to pin them down to specific fears.

Where the anxiety is fixed to a specific cause it is described as *bound*. So fear of loss or unemployment, if real, would come into this category.

Phobia – is a fear which has become pathological. Whatever is feared usually produces a marked physiological response which may be long-standing.

There are literally hundreds of things that one might develop phobias about, but the common factor to each is the strong need for avoidance of the feared object.

- *claustrophobia* – is a flight to open spaces.
- *agoraphobia* – is flight to a closed or secure place.
- *schizophrenia* – is an extreme phobic response which is a flight from the outside world and includes alienation from one's own body.

Coping with phobia

Studies show that phobias tend to arise in persons who have been over-protected by over-possessive parents, but this is not the sole cause.

Phobias have been coped with on a number of levels. In the absence of treatment, various self-help techniques have been tried, but where these do not work the reactions and responses to phobia become increasingly uncontrollable:

Level **1**:
Attempt at self-control, joking
about the situation, crying,
swearing, boasting, trying to
think it through, talking the
problem out, and working off
the frustration.

Level **2**:
Withdrawing by:

• *dissociation* – becoming amnesiac about the problem, using drugs to help forget and depersonalising the problem.

• *displacement of aggression* – by using aversion techniques, prejudices, acquiring other phobias, and the use of counter-phobic attitudes like walking on or counting squares or lines.

Substitution:

• *of symbols* – such as compulsions and rituals.

• by *aggression of self or part of self*, self-injury such as cutting the flesh, physical abasement, self-intoxication and drug-taking.

Level **3**:
Outbursts of aggressive energy
from time to time, more or less
disorganised, including on
occasions violent assaults on
others; convulsions, and
extreme panic attacks.

Level **4**:
The increased disorganisation
of the personality becomes
more apparent.

Level **5**:
Total disintegration of the
personality.

- Fortunately, most phobics are treated for their phobias at levels one and two so do not progress to the levels beyond.

- Identifying fears, anxieties and phobias at an early stage and then dealing with them promptly is important to the person's well-being.

- Treatment may be by some form of desensitising and/or counselling to eradicate the underlying problem.

Prevalence of phobias

The most common phobia is the familiar agoraphobia, experienced by 10-50% of phobics, and is a problem particularly associated with early adulthood. Ten percent of phobics have some form of social phobia acquired during the stressful years of adolescence.

Five to 15% of phobics fear animals, usually from childhood; 20% of phobics have a phobia about inanimate objects (contact with particular materials, and so on), these phobias being acquired at any age; 15-20% of phobics fear illness or injury, and this phobia is usually acquired in middle age.

Across the range of phobias, the vast majority of sufferers are women.

Mistaken assumption

However painful and distressing
your symptoms may currently
be; however irrational and
inexplicable the phobic
response may seem to you at
this moment; however complete
your loss of mental and/or
physical control in the phobic
situation may appear, these are
not to be taken as symptoms of
a serious mental illness. Nor as
the early warnings of an
impending nervous breakdown.

Robert Sharp, David Lewis

Circumstantial evidence!

People are always blaming their circumstances for what they are. I don't believe in circumstances. The people who get on in this world are the people who get up and look for the circumstances they want, and if they can't find them, make them.

George Bernard Shaw

Unemployment

For many people today,
unemployment is an ever-
present prospect or actually
experienced. A number of
studies have shown that even
the anticipation of redundancy
causes people to attend their
doctor's surgery. They go with
all the familiar complaints, but
the root cause is fear – fear of
the unknown.

Where fairly large-scale redundancies take place, we see a rise in heart disease, alcoholism, smoking and drinking-related diseases, excessive use of prescribed drugs and the illicit use of others, suicide, attempted suicide, and an increase in psychiatric admissions.

In order for people to be happy in their work, these things are needed: They must be fit for it; *They must not have too much of it;* And they must have a sense of success in it.

John Ruskin

Isolation

Part of the unemployment problem is the loss of social contact with work colleagues. Surveys have shown that where people perceive themselves to be isolated and alone, and of course where this is also a fact, they develop a whole range of poor health problems – with heart disease way out in front in the statistics. Where there is integration, companionship and fellowship, the health risks diminish and health improves.

Belonging

The *sense of coherence* is a
global orientation that
expresses the extent to which
one has a pervasive, enduring
though dynamic feeling of
confidence that one's internal
and external environments are
predictable, and that there is a
high probability that things will
work out as well as can
reasonably be expected.
Aaron Antonovsky

Hopeless and helpless!

The person with a weak sense of coherence meets the adaptive requirement with a sense of helplessness, which becomes a self-fulfilling prophecy: he or she sees the life change as not making sense and therefore is incapable of successful adaptation.

Aaron Antonovsky

Small town, big rewards!

The healthiest lifestyle is that
of a citizen living in a small
caring community where
problems are shared and
relationships developed,
established and respected.
Dr Vernon Coleman

Coping efforts

Definitions of coping must include *efforts* to manage stressful demands, regardless of outcome. This means that no one strategy is considered inherently better than any other.

Richard S. Lazarus, Susan Folkman

Hidden resources

Potentiation – the calling up
of hitherto potential resources
and thereby enriching
one's repertoire – is precisely
a possible consequence
of tension.

A. A. Monjan, M. I. Collector

Getting the act together

Coping consists of
cognitive and behavioural
efforts to manage specific
external and/or internal
demands that are appraised as
taxing or exceeding the
resources of the person.
Richard S. Lazarus, Susan Folkman

Poor management

Poor tension management leads to the stress syndrome and movement toward dis-ease on the continuum. Good tension management pushes on toward health ease.

Aaron Antonovsky

Reducing the risk

Meeting, sharing, taking part, play a central role in maintaining the social support. Other aspects of the health advantage of church attendance can also be readily understood and easily explained. For example, evangelical churchgoers are less likely to be alcohol drinkers or smokers, thus eliminating some chemical stressors and lowering the risk factors for serious ill-health such as heart disease and cancer.

Quality of life

The quality as well as the quantity of the relationship involved is important. Being totally involved with others in the home and the community is of prime importance; so belonging to clubs and societies has *physical* advantages as well as the anticipated social outcomes.

But there is more! Social psychologist Richard Totman says: 'People holding religious beliefs and regular churchgoers enjoy better health than non-believers and non-attenders.' Why? 'Belonging to a religious community offers the individual a powerful source of social support through opportunities to meet regularly, the sharing of commitments and other beliefs and their expression in the established rituals and liturgies that lie at the heart of all faiths.'

O what peace we often forfeit.
O what needless pain we bear,
All because we do not carry
Everything to God in prayer.
Joseph Scriven

Making reality!

If men define situations as real,
they are real in their
consequences.

W. I. Thomas

With good in mind

On the whole, it is of greatest importance for a man to heed what thoughts he entertains, as what company he keeps; bad thoughts are as infectious as bad company, and good thoughts solace, instruct and entertain the mind, like good company.

Mason

Cultivation of character

... if we wish to conquer
undesirable emotional
tendencies in ourselves, we
must assiduously, and in the
first instance cold-bloodedly, go
through the outward
movements of those contrary
dispositions which we prefer to
cultivate. The reward of
persistence will infallibly come,
in the fading of sullenness or
depression, and the advent of
real cheerfulness and
kindliness in their stead.
Professor William James

Individual health status

Whether an individual is single, married, divorced or bereaved, all have a positive or negative effect on our health. Richard Totman states that 'social support has been consistently linked, through research, with a low risk of numerous physical and psychiatric illnesses, and with favourable prognosis in sick patients. . . . Social support has been studied in relation to a wide range of physical illnesses, including heart disease, cancer, hypertension and respiratory disorders and there is good evidence that it exerts a favourable influence on health in all of these.'

. . . do not worry about your
life, what you will eat or drink;
or about your body, what you
will wear. . . . Who of you
by worrying can add a
single hour to his life?
Matthew 6:25, 27

I have learned the secret of
being content in any and
every situation.
Philippians 4:12

Ye fearful saints,
fresh courage take;
The clouds ye so much dread
Are big with mercy
and will break
In blessings on your head.
William Cowper

Personal choices

In the coming decades, the most important determinants of health and longevity will be the personal choices made by each individual. This is both frightening for those who wish to avoid such responsibility and exciting for those who desire some control over their own destiny.

William H. Foege
(former Assistant Secretary, US Dept of Health and Human Services)

Positively healthy!

I became convinced that creativity, the will to live, hope, faith, and love have biochemical significance and contribute strongly to healing and well-being.

Norman Cousins

Health is . . . 'a *modus vivendi*
enabling imperfect men to
achieve a rewarding and not too
painful existence while they
cope with an imperfect world.'
Rene J. Dubos

Overwhelmed

... ill health ... appears to
occur when an individual
exists in a life situation which
places demands upon him that
are excessive in terms of his
ability to meet them.
S. Wolf, H. Goodell

Lifestyle stressors

Some of our common lifestyle habits impair brain function and come under the heading of chemical stressors. These include: illegal and, sometimes, prescribed *drugs*; *alcohol*; *smoking*; and even *caffeine* intake.

● **Drugs** can depress, exhilarate and distort perceptions of time, distance and reality, depending on which drugs are used. Long-term use of prescribed drugs may cause similar effects.

● **Alcohol** is a nervous-system depressant acting in the first instance on the frontal lobes and progressing with quantity to depress other brain centres. Alcohol causes stickiness of the red blood cells which makes a sludgy circulatory system.

- **Smoking** constricts blood vessels, making the heart and lungs work harder, contributing to a rise in blood pressure, and replaces essential oxygen with harmful carbon monoxide and carbon dioxide. Nicotine stimulates and depresses the nerves.

• **Caffeine** – the active ingredient in tea, coffee and cola drinks, chocolate and over-the-counter painkillers – is a stimulant that works together with nicotine in constricting blood vessels, and is also psychologically connected with smoking and a high-paced lifestyle.

Type A and Type B behaviours

Two American cardiologists – Meyer Friedman and Ray Rosenman – researching the concept of coronary-prone personality, concluded that personality traits contribute to heart disease, and have a strong link to everyday stress.

Analysing the traits of people attending their coronary clinics, the doctors discovered that there were two distinct types of personality that emerged. They called these traits Type A and Type B personalities. It was particularly noticed that the Type A personalities were the coronary-prone. Type B personalities also developed heart disease, but with nothing like the same frequency.

A whole range of behaviour traits was identified for both of these groups, allowing a fair degree of accuracy in predicting who might develop heart disease in the short and long term if the lifestyle remained unchanged.

Further experiments showed that modifying or changing the lifestyle behaviour characteristics of Type A to those of Type B markedly reduced the heart disease risk. The behaviour traits are summarised as follows:

Type A behaviours

- Vocal explosiveness and accentuation of speech.

- Rapidity in eating and movement.

- Unrestrained impatience.

- Taking on too much and trying to think and do a variety of things simultaneously by choice.

- Difficulty in getting away from self-interest.

- Guilt on relaxing.

- Insensitive to, or unaware of, surroundings.

- More concerned with having than being.

- Aggression and hostility surfacing as competitiveness.

- Characteristic gestures or nervous habits.

- Attributing all success to oneself.

- Reducing everything to statistics and numbers.

Type B behaviours

- Free of all Type A habits.
- No time urgency or impatience.
- Uncompetitive and without hostility.
- Plays for fun and not to demonstrate superiority.
- Relaxes without guilt.

Stress and personality

Type As are engaged in a struggle for control. . . . Pattern A behaviour is a strategy for coping with uncontrollable stress; enhanced performance reflects an attempt to assert and maintain control after its loss has been threatened.

D. C. Glass

Stress-proofing

We do not usually wait until the storms come to get our house weatherproof. The storms merely test what we have prepared. Likewise, we should not wait until the stressors come before making our preparations.

For most of us a lifestyle change would get us back into balance and able to cope when the stormy stressors arrive. In order to do this we should have some well-laid plans. These plans must include a regimen of healthy living. In addition to the general rules of good health, such as fresh air, sunshine, exercise, temperance and good rest, there are some specific areas of health that might need attention.

Nerve food

In order to function well, the nerve cells should be serviced by the B range of vitamins (1, 2, 3, 5, 6, 12). Each has a specific role to play – strengthening the cell wall or the nerve sheath, combining with other substances in the fluid of the cell, and helping with the transmission of nerve impulses.

A diet that provides these vitamins will help to stress-proof the body.

A winning formula

The B vitamins can be found in: whole-wheat, wholemeal, wheat germ and yeast products. As vitamin B is water-soluble, the body does not retain more of it than it needs.

Oxygen, along with vitamin B and enzymes in our food, provides us with nervous energy. If either oxygen or vitamin B is deficient from the formula, the individual will feel irritable, ratty and tense. Providing the proper balance will usually alleviate these symptoms.

A quick boost

If a quick boost to the system is required, then a course of *Brewers' Yeast* or *vitamin B complex* tablets will help. By the time these supplements are finished, the natural sources of B vitamins should be part of your regular diet.

WARNING:
If you are on antidepressant drugs prescribed by your doctor as MAOs you will have been told to avoid certain foods and the above supplements.

Oh, sugar!

If the symptoms do remain there is one factor which might be disturbing the equilibrium – *sugar*. Sugar (of whatever kind) uses up vitamin B as it burns or metabolises in the body. Excess sugar can therefore deplete the body, and the nervous system in particular, of essential B vitamins. This includes the 'hidden' sugars of ready-to-eat foods which might not be so obvious – glucose, dextrose, fructose, maltose and lactose. Honey is no substitute in this instance as it too burns B vitamins.

The four sources of
self-esteem are:

- our *achievements* and
  accomplishments

- the *exercise of power*, *control*
  and *influence*

- being *valued*, *loved* and
  cared about

- having *behaviours* consistent
  with our *values* and *beliefs*

These may be met through our
family, personal life, work, and
other experiences and
relationships.

Self-worth

(self-esteem)

At the heart of many of the problems that face us is the feeling that we are failures to ourselves, our families, and to society. A sense of worthlessness pervades which can be hard to shake off. This is especially true during the withdrawal/confusion and adjustment phases of the change and crisis sequence. The following exercise may be of help.

- List **ten** things you like about yourself. These need only be simple things like hairstyle, dress sense, smile, and so on.

- List **five** things others like about you. This can be anything good that you might have heard and that gives you pleasure to think about.

- List your talents. These may be formal qualifications, hobbies or general skills. The number is not important.

• What in your estimation makes a person valuable? A number of character traits may come to mind, but try to narrow them down to one and then ask:

1. Is it true of you?

2. If this is not true of you, what could you do to make it so?

• Write a short paragraph explaining why you are a valuable person.

• Review what you have written regarding yourself from your self-appraisal.

• Write out the words of encouragement below on a small card and carry it in your purse or wallet:

Peace is what I leave with you; it is my own peace that I give you.

I do not give it as the world does.

Do not be worried and upset; do not be afraid.

John 14:27, GNB

This verse should help to put your worth into its proper context as you appreciate the extra help that is available to you.

Deep breathing

The brain and nerve cells (along with all the tissues of the body) require oxygen, the intake of which can be restricted by lifestyle habits such as smoking or physical inactivity.

A deep breathing regime may help you to get back on track.

The average adult breathing rate when at rest is between 14 and 20 breaths a minute. If we breathe out hard and then take in a deep breath, we can draw in about eight times as much new air as in our resting breath.

In the initial stages of trying to make the deep breathing technique habitual, it is best to stand with feet slightly apart, maintaining a good balance. Then proceed as follows:

- Loosen or remove constricting clothing and let your fingertips hold on to the ribs below the diaphragm.

- Take a deep breath in, filling the top and bottom of the lungs. As you breathe in, gently pull the lower ribs out – this straightens the diaphragm, rather like opening a pair of bellows.

- Hold the breath for the count of 6 or 8, then release all the breath slowly, forcing the air out and using your hands to gently push the sides of the chest until you think there is nothing left to come.

- Give a cough – this helps to flip the diaphragm and release the residual carbon dioxide at the base of the lungs.

- Repeat the exercise 6-10 times at least twice a day, reducing the amount if light-headed.

As you get used to the deep breathing there will be no need to use your hands or cough. Breathing deeply and using your stomach muscles to help fill the lungs will soon become second nature and you will be able to use the technique anytime and anywhere.

Aerobics

You might like to follow your deep breathing with exercises designed to stimulate your heart and lung activity. These exercises are called *aerobic* and include many kinds of popular sports. You may have an aerobic exercise class near you.

As you acquire the habit of deep breathing – including a range of aerobic activities – you will be contributing to your stress-proofing as well as gaining good general fitness.

Rest

The most effective answer to the problem of stress is to minimise it as far as possible. But rest alone is not sufficient, although useful. As Dr Selye affirms – *rest is not enough*. He says, 'Many people believe that, after they have exposed themselves to very stressful activities, a rest can restore them to where they were before. This is false. Experiments on animals have clearly shown that each exposure *leaves an indelible scar, in that it uses up reserves of adaptability which cannot be replaced*.'

Nor is exercise necessarily the answer to a mind needing rest. Often those whose minds are stressed by the pressure of their work seek relief in exercise, thinking that a change will relieve the tired mind. But if the body is not accustomed to exercise, the exhilaration of the mind is then counterbalanced by abused muscles, thus further stressing the body. Relaxation of body and mind are needed *together*.

In relaxing mood

There is a rhythm in the
electrical activity of the brain
cells that varies according to
our daily programme over
which – to a large extent – we
can exercise conscious control.
These states are:

beta – 13-30 cycles per second,
the normal conscious state

alpha – 8-12 cycles per second,
the relaxed state

theta – 4-7 cycles per second, the state before sleep

delta – 0.5-3 cycles per second, sleep or unconsciousness.

As you can see, during the course of a day we move up and down through the cycles influenced by our physical and mental states, the weather, our food, environment and activities.

Alpha control

In relaxation we aim to spend beneficial time in the *alpha state*. Care needs to be taken in choosing the appropriate relaxation techniques, as there are hidden dangers in many of these – including the most popular ones, such as meditation and hypnosis.

In the alpha state our breathing is slower and shallower, the heart rate slows, less oxygen is used and less carbon dioxide is eliminated, and our blood chemistry changes.

Relaxation

A simple but effective way to achieve total relaxation is to relax progressively the various muscle groups of the body. First, decide when and where your main relaxation period will be and create the right ambience – dim lighting, warm surroundings, gentle background music (avoiding tapes with subliminal messages). Loosen or remove tight clothing and lie on a comfortable carpet with support to the neck and lower back, or on your bed. Familiarise yourself with and follow these instructions:

1. Clench both fists. Notice the pull on your wrist, around your elbow and even up in the shoulder. This is extreme tension.

2. Open your fist. Immediately the muscles of hand, forearm, arm and shoulder release their contraction – and in doing so the tension is gone. (Perform exercises 1 and 2 three times.)

3. Next bend the toes and feet downward and push or stretch with the heels. Notice the pull in your ankles, feet, hips and thighs, but particularly in the calves of the legs. This is muscular tension.

4. Now let go and the muscular tension disappears. (Perform exercises 3 and 4 three times.)

5. The last exercise is for the muscles of the neck, throat and face. First close the eyes as tightly as you can. At the same time press the lips together and bite hard with the jaws. This contracts the muscles of your eyes, forehead, mouth, jaw and neck. You can feel the tension and even hear it ringing in your ears.

6. Now let go with your jaw and face. If your head falls on one side, let it – you are learning to release tension, learning to relax. (Perform exercises 5 and 6 three times.)

As you do each exercise note where the tensions are and then relax. Relaxation is not achieved until all the tensions are gone. You should not expect that the exercises will be totally successful on the first few attempts. Practice makes perfect. After a while you will no longer need to exercise each of these muscle groups, for as you settle to relax you will feel your tension ease away. Breathe gently in, and as you breathe out let your tensions go with your breath.

Relax to music!

Music produces alterations in *physiology*.... Soothing music can produce ... relaxation in which autonomic, immune, endocrine and neuropeptide systems are altered.

Cathie E. Guzzetta

Music exalts each joy,
allays each grief,
Expels disease,
softens every pain,
Subdues the rage of poison,
and the plague.

John Armstrong